DODD, MEAD WONDERS BOOKS

WONDERS OF ALLIGATORS AND CROCODILES by Wyatt Blassingame
WONDERS OF ANIMAL ARCHITECTURE by Sigmund A. Lavine
WONDERS OF ANIMAL NURSERIES by Jacquelyn Berrill
WONDERS OF BARNACLES by Arnold Ross and William K. Emerson
WONDERS OF THE BAT WORLD by Sigmund A. Lavine
WONDERS BEYOND THE SOLAR SYSTEM by Rocco Feravolo
WONDERS OF THE BISON WORLD by Sigmund A. Lavine and Vincent Scuro
WONDERS OF THE CACTUS WORLD by Sigmund A. Lavine
WONDERS OF CARIBOU by Jim Rearden
WONDERS OF THE DINOSAUR WORLD by William H. Matthews III
WONDERS OF THE EAGLE WORLD by Sigmund A. Lavine
WONDERS OF THE FLY WORLD by Sigmund A. Lavine
WONDERS OF FROGS AND TOADS by Wyatt Blassingame
WONDERS OF GEESE AND SWANS by Thomas D. Fegely
WONDERS OF GEMS by Richard M. Pearl
WONDERS OF GRAVITY by Rocco Feravolo
WONDERS OF THE HAWK WORLD by Sigmund A. Lavine
WONDERS OF HERBS by Sigmund A. Lavine
WONDERS OF HUMMINGBIRDS by Hilda Simon
WONDERS OF THE KELP FOREST by Joseph E. Brown
WONDERS OF LLAMAS by Roger Perry
WONDERS OF LIONS by George and Kay Schaller
WONDERS OF MATHEMATICS by Rocco Feravolo
WONDERS OF MEASUREMENT by Owen S. Lieberg
WONDERS OF THE MONKEY WORLD by Jacquelyn Berrill
WONDERS OF THE MOSQUITO WORLD by Phil Ault
WONDERS OF THE OWL WORLD by Sigmund A. Lavine
WONDERS OF THE PELICAN WORLD by Joseph J. Cook and Ralph W. Schreiber
WONDERS OF PRAIRIE DOGS by G. Earl Chace
WONDERS OF THE PRONGHORN by G. Earl Chace
WONDERS OF RACCOONS by Wyatt Blassingame
WONDERS OF ROCKS AND MINERALS by Richard M. Pearl
WONDERS OF SAND by Christie McFall
WONDERS OF SEA GULLS by Elizabeth Anne and Ralph W. Schreiber
WONDERS OF SEALS AND SEA LIONS by Joseph E. Brown
WONDERS OF SOUND by Rocco Feravolo
WONDERS OF THE SPIDER WORLD by Sigmund A. Lavine
WONDERS OF SPONGES by Morris K. Jacobson and Rosemary K. Pang
WONDERS OF STARFISH by Morris K. Jacobson and William K. Emerson
WONDERS OF STONES by Christie McFall
WONDERS OF TERRARIUMS by Sigmund A. Lavine
WONDERS OF THE TREE WORLD by Margaret Cosgrove
WONDERS OF THE TURTLE WORLD by Wyatt Blassingame
WONDERS OF WILD DUCKS by Thomas D. Fegely
WONDERS OF THE WOODS AND DESERT AT NIGHT by Jacquelyn Berrill
WONDERS OF THE WORLD OF THE ALBATROSS by Harvey and Mildred Fisher
WONDERS OF THE WORLD OF BEARS by Bernadine Bailey
WONDERS OF THE WORLD OF HORSES by Sigmund A. Lavine and Brigid Casey
WONDERS OF THE WORLD OF SHELLS by Morris K. Jacobson and William K. Emerson
WONDERS OF THE WORLD OF WOLVES by Jacquelyn Berrill
WONDERS OF YOUR SENSES by Margaret Cosgrove

Wonders of the Pronghorn

G. EARL CHACE

Illustrated with photographs by the author

DODD, MEAD & COMPANY · NEW YORK

In memory of my parents,
CAPTAIN HENRY B. and BELLE M. CHACE,
who tolerated my pets and never discouraged
my interest in nature

ACKNOWLEDGMENTS

The true source of information concerning any animal is in the field with the subject. However, it takes hours, days, and often years to discover and learn much about them—and there are so many animals. Therefore, I'd like to acknowledge those people who spent many hours watching pronghorns, those who acted to save the pronghorns from vanishing, those landowners upon whose land the wild pronghorns feed, and those from whom I exacted information because they knew things I didn't. To all of them—thank you!

The photographs on pages 19, 28 (bottom), and 39 courtesy of the South Dakota Department of Game, Fish and Parks. All other photographs are by the author.

1 2 3 4 5 6 7 8 9 10

Library of Congress Cataloging in Publication Data
Chace, G Earl.
Wonders of the pronghorn.

Bibliography: p.
Includes index.
SUMMARY: Describes the physical characteristics and habits of the North American pronghorn antelope and discusses its adaptation to a prairie environment and the effects of civilization on its well-being.
1. Pronghorn antelopes—Juvenile literature.
[1. Pronghorn antelopes. 2. Antelopes] I. Title.
QL737.U52C48 599'.7358 77-6490
ISBN 0-396-07480-4

Contents

Chest and facial markings vary from one pronghorn to another.

I
The Pronghorn

The sunny prairies of western North America seem almost barren of wildlife when crossed by today's travelers. They are indeed barren if compared to the types and quantities of wildlife listed in the journals of the early explorers of this continent. The practically endless bison herds no longer exist. The millions upon millions of prairie dog mounds do not dot the prairie for as far as the eye can see, nor must one fear an encounter with the giant grizzly bear or roving wolf pack. Even the deer and elk seek the safety and seclusion of any shrub- and tree-covered areas when the sun shines. Today's travelers might feel they are driving past miles and miles of barbed wire fences enclosing only domestic cattle and sheep. However, one sizable, visible, sun-loving, big game creature still exists in appreciable numbers on the prairie. It is called the North American pronghorn.

It may take a sharp eye to see a solitary buck standing silhouetted on top of a grassy mound at some distance from the highway. It will thrill even the most casual traveler to see an entire, alerted herd of pronghorns running across the grasslands and disappearing over the top of a distant rise. Their snow-white rumps flash in the sun like reflecting mirrors. Their flowing gallop covers the ground at a smooth but high speed. The entire herd, like a school of fish, changes directions and responds as one.

When observed closely, the pronghorn is a magnificent animal. It is deerlike in appearance, but smaller. A male weighs

Horns and facial markings of a prime buck

about 100 to 130 pounds, a female about 20 pounds less. The pronghorn stands about three feet high at the shoulder and is about four feet long, not counting the short, four- or five-inch tail. It has large black eyes, a long narrow face, and long ears. Both male and female have horns. Those of the male, or buck, may reach fourteen or more inches in length (the present record is 20⅛ inches) and have one branch or prong, which gives the animal its name. The horns of the female, or doe, are never branched, are much smaller than the horns of the male, and are occasionally missing altogether. The long legs of the pronghorn are slim, almost spindly in appearance, but are probably the most efficient running legs to be found on the prairie.

A golden tan provides the basic color of the pelage, or coat, which is trimmed with black and white. The white forms a large circular patch on the rump, covers the underparts of the body,

and marks off two rectangular areas on either side of the animal. It also colors the lips and lower portions of the cheeks and chin. The chest has a white shieldlike design, and the front of the neck has two broad, white bands. White also covers the top of the head, between the horns and around the base of the ears. The black color covers the horns, nose, eyes, and the inside of the mouth. The male also has black patches on the cheeks, near the back of its jaws. A small amount of dark brown marks a crest or mane on the upper neck, but is normally seen only when the pronghorn becomes angry or excited. The vividness of these colors varies somewhat from season to season as the animal sheds and changes from summer to winter pelage or vice versa. The chest and facial designs also vary enough from one individual to another to enable scientific observers to recognize a specific pronghorn after several days of study.

As old as the prairie itself, the pronghorn is one of the original members of the North American fauna. Many of the early explorers of this continent mentioned the animal in their journals. They used the meat for food and the hides for covering, but they were not sure of what type of animal it was.

This buck is not frightened, but decides to leave anyway. Note the circular rump patch.

The American elk shares parts of the range of the pronghorn antelope. Like all members of the deer family, it has antlers rather than horns.

Coronado saw pronghorns in the year 1540 and thought of them as deer with white markings. Lewis and Clark, on their expedition across the northern part of the country in 1804, referred to them as goats or antelope. They thoughtfully brought one back, and a zoologist named George Ord gave it the scientific name of *Antilocapra americana*—or, translated from Latin, "American antelope goat." Zebulon Pike saw the pronghorn on his travels through Kansas in 1906 and called it the cabree, after the French Canadians. Various plains Indian tribes, such as the Sioux, had their own names—*tahtohkahnah* and *tahca*. The early settlers called it either goat, antelope, pronghorn, or prongbuck. One reason for the various names lies in the animal's resemblance to both deer and the true antelope of the Old World.

Millions of years ago, the true antelope, the deer, and the pronghorn may have shared common ancestry, but the modern animals are different. All three are called cloven-hoofed ungulates, meaning that they are hoofed and that their hooves appear to be split into two parts. However, the most obvious and quickest method of distinguishing the three animals is by looking at their "horns."

Deer horns are more accurately called antlers. They are made entirely of bone, have many branches or tines, and are completely shed and regrown each year. The true antelope has horns which, like cow horns, have a horny or keratin coating. These are never branched and never shed. The pronghorn or prongbuck, as its name implies, has a branch or prong on each horn of the adult male. The pronghorn sheds and renews only the outer keratin cover of its horns. This heavy cover or sheath encloses a bony spike or permanent core which is never shed.

The horns of the pronghorn are not round and smooth like those of the cow, but bumpy, warty looking, and slightly flattened. When they are shed, sometime between mid-October and mid-November, they usually fall off separately, often several days apart. Unlike the deer, which makes an effort to rid itself of its loosened antlers at shedding time, the pronghorn seems to pay no attention to its horns. One day, when lowering its head to bite at a clump of grass, one or both of its horn sheaths simply fall off.

The preparation for shedding takes place over a period of weeks before it actually occurs. Each new sheath begins to grow on the inner bony spike long before the old sheath falls off. Oddly enough, this growth begins at the tip of the unshed spike and progresses both up and down, with the prong forming at the location of the tip of the spike. Perhaps it is the growing of the new sheath that loosens the old.

Both the inner surface of the sheath and the outer surface of

the spike are slightly hairy, which gives rise to the story that the sheaths are made of congealed hairs. Although the hairs are present, the outer sheath is, like the cow's horn, a deposit of keratin. Keratin is the same material that fingernails are made of, and not compressed hair.

Every new sheath is slightly longer, heavier, and thicker, and has a longer prong than the one just shed. The old one, which drops to the ground, is rarely found because rainwater gradually softens the material and it begins to decompose—or else the small animals, such as rats, mice, or porcupines, eat it.

It is extremely difficult to stand upon the prairie and visualize it once covered with a great inland sea. The presence of numerous marine fossils tells us that it once was. Equally difficult is to imagine this sea drained off and the place it once covered turned into a lush, swampy area inhabited by prehistoric reptiles and mammals. Again, fossils indicate that this actually happened. Fossils also show that the swamp dried up and a forest grew, and

Opposite: *The horns and top of the head of a pronghorn shot by a hunter.* Right: *A close-up of the inner bony spike*

finally, our eyes show us that this same land is now a tremendous, rolling sea of grass.

During these changes, a small mammal developed that was destined to evolve into the beautiful animal we know as the American pronghorn. Just as fossils have recorded the changes in the land, so have they recorded related changes in the pronghorn—all of which took place over a period of about 20 million years.

The great change from a vast sea, to a tropical swamp, to the cool, high, semiarid grassland was caused by the gradual uplifting of the Rocky Mountain chain and its eastern slopes. As the land rose, the sea drained off and the air grew cooler. The mountains blocked most of the predominant western winds and the moisture they brought from the Pacific Ocean. Not enough moisture fell to support the forest, so it died off. The eastern slopes were left to the shallow-rooted grasses that can survive with little rainfall and drying winds.

The little swamp-dwelling ancestor of the modern pronghorn

A grazing buck

A beautiful pronghorn doe

had to change to exist. The early fossils of antelopelike creatures show that many changes occurred and many species evolved. Some had four horns; some had curled horns; some had twisted horns. Some animals were quite large and others were small—all, except our presentday species, were unable to make the changes necessary for the new conditions and have become extinct. Scientists have named this family Antilocapridae, and the single remaining species *Antilocapra americana*, the only one of its kind. It has no living relatives and, according to fossil records, has changed little, or not at all during the past million years. Neither are there any records of it on any other continent. It is one hundred percent American.

The pronghorn is remarkably well equipped to survive in the open. Its highly developed eyes can see for miles. Its fleetness and endurance enable it to outrun most predators. Its ears and nostrils detect either sound or scent in ample time for flight. Its coloration gives it reasonable camouflage against a background of prairie grass, and its timidity sends it bounding at the least sign of trouble. Even its young, the fawns, can stand up in approximately one-half hour or less, walk in an hour or so, and outrun a man at only three days of age. The pronghorn is also basically gregarious by nature and enjoys the company of others of its kind. It has a system whereby any individual can, by odor, sight, or sound, relay warnings that will instantly alert the entire herd.

The pronghorn lives in an immense area that embraces portions of several biomes—the high, short-grass prairie, the hot, dry desert, and the very high, intermountain plains. A biome is a biological area of such altitude, climate, temperature, rainfall, and soil conditions that only plants and animals equipped for these conditions can live there.

To watch a pronghorn closely, one would doubt that such a delicate-looking creature could survive in its harsh surround-

ings. Its range extends from southern Canada down into northern Mexico, and from the Rocky Mountains almost to the Missouri and Mississippi rivers. The altitude in the east is about 2,000 feet, and near the Rockies it reaches almost 10,000 feet. Pronghorns can be found at an altitude of 10,000 in some of the prairielike valleys between mountain ranges. Because of the mountains and altitude, much of this area is semidesert, and in the Southwest, true desert. Without the buffering effect of moisture in the air, these biomes are subjected to fast and great changes in temperature. It can be 100 degrees Fahrenheit at noon and 50 degrees at night. Seasonal changes vary from 115 degrees in summer to, on the more northerly, higher ranges, 40 degrees below zero. Summer moisture can arrive as torrential rains that produce flash floods or large hail. Winters often bring cold, strong winds and blizzards and thick blankets of snow with deep drifts that cover much of the available food.

Delicate-looking or not, the pronghorn is hardy. Its sleek, seemingly inadequate coat is composed of long, brittle, air-filled hairs that provide ample insulation. Furthermore, each hair is capable of being raised or depressed to provide different degrees of insulation or ventilation, depending upon the temperature.

The short-grass prairie of South Dakota where pronghorns live

Southern Wyoming has much desertlike country where pronghorns manage to eke out a living.

Cactus pads and weeds provide sufficient moisture when the prairie dries up, and a modified digestive tract allows the pronghorn to eat plants that would make other plains creatures ill. And, to avoid predators, the pronghorn depends upon speed and endurance made possible by several enlarged, internal organs.

Antilocapra americana americana is the predominant subspecies in North America, making up almost 90 percent of all existing pronghorns. There are, however, four other subspecies that live on the edges of the main range. *A. a. oregona*, or the Oregon pronghorn, is found in the eastern parts of that state. *A. a. mexicana* is found not only in northeast Mexico, but also up into southeast Arizona, southwest New Mexico, and into Texas. *A. a. sonoriensis* lives in Sonora, Mexico, and in southern Arizona, and finally, *A. a. peninsularis* is found in Baja California. The average observer can tell these subspecies apart essentially only by knowing from where they come. There are subtle differences in size and color only. They are all North American pronghorns.

American bison and their young

According to the reports of the early explorers of North America, there were once as many pronghorns as there were bison, estimated to have numbered 60 million. Some explorers claimed the pronghorns were even more numerous. Like bison, the pronghorns became the target of hunters who needed both meat and hides for their sustenance, and their population dropped until it reached a point dangerously close to extinction. An alerted public grew alarmed that this was happening, and just as with the bison, societies for the preservation and protection of the pronghorn came into existence. One after another, the various pronghorn states began establishing protective areas where the few remaining animals could hope to stage a comeback. A few examples are the Charles Sheldon National Refuge in Nevada, the Hart Mountain Refuge in Oregon, Custer State Park and Wind Cave National Park in South Dakota, Yellowstone National Park in Wyoming, and the National Bison Range in Montana.

Not only did the various states begin to set up protective areas,

they also began to count, or estimate carefully, the number of pronghorns to be found within their boundaries. They did this every year. They also established laws prohibiting hunting of pronghorns, the results of which have been gratifying.

The following statistics, for example, were established by the state of South Dakota. In 1850 there were an estimated 700,000 pronghorns in the state. In 1909, they were considered to be extinct east of the Missouri River, with very few remaining in the western half of the state. In 1911, South Dakota enacted a law prohibiting hunting the animals. In 1924, it was estimated that only 680 of them inhabited the entire state. In 1941, the estimate rose to 11,000. In 1942, the state began to issue a designated number of pronghorn hunting permits for the first time in thirty-one years, yet in 1965, the estimated pronghorn population in South Dakota had risen to 28,000. In 1975, the count reached 43,083. Although 12,139 hunting licenses were issued, only 10,031 pronghorns were killed. If the birthrate runs according to expectation, a substantial increase can be foreseen. Game biologists in South Dakota, and all pronghorn states, watch statistics carefully, in order to attain a balance between food supply and pronghorn population.

Pronghorns running from the sound of the plane as the state of South Dakota makes an aerial head count

2

Adaptations to Prairie Existence

For thousands of years, the pronghorn has had to contend with many animal enemies. These years of avoiding them have shaped both its habits and body into the best possible defense characteristics.

The pronghorn lives in an area where it can usually see to the horizon at all points of the compass, so its eyes have become the first line of defense. If it can see trouble approaching soon enough, it can normally avoid it. The pronghorn has large eyes, larger even than those of a horse, which is a much bigger animal. They are set neither on the side nor directly on the front of the head, but rather on the corners. They are set in raised, bony sockets which form a protective wall against the sharp twigs and branches of the brushes and shrubs that it uses as food. They are dark colored, which overcomes some of the strong ultraviolet light of high altitude and unshaded prairie. But most important, the pronghorn can, without turning its head, see straight ahead or off to either side with almost equal ability. The location and size of its eyes enable it to cover great areas at a glance, and to see small objects at long distances. Some authorities compare pronghorn vision to man's when aided by an 8-power binocular.

Any movement or change on the familiar prairie seems to be noticed at once, and if it does not present an immediate threat, the pronghorn will stand and stare before deciding whether to run or not. A moving man can be spotted quickly at a distance

A young buck shows pronghorn curiosity. Note the facial designs and the placement of the eyes.

of approximately two miles. Occasionally a strange object which does not appear threatening excites the curiosity of the pronghorn, and it slowly and carefully approaches in an effort to understand. Hunters have made use of this trait by attaching a rag to a shrub and letting it flap gently in the wind. Although such bait has worked, it is quite time-consuming and is not always successful. The pronghorn tempers its curiosity with extreme caution.

The pronghorn remains active after dark. It wanders about its range, changing its resting places, or engaging in other pronghorn pursuits. Nighttime has always been an active time for predators also, and with reduced vision, the pronghorn has to depend more on scent and sound for warning. Its large, mobile ears can readily detect suspicious noises above the usual

sounds of the prairie, and they turn quickly toward the sound for better reception. The pronghorn's sense of smell is also acute. It not only warns of approaching enemies, such as the coyote or bobcat, but aids in finding the highly scented sage and other plants upon which it feeds. Smell also becomes important during the mating season, when the dominant males mark out the invisible boundaries of their territories.

The pronghorn has several sets of scent glands distributed about its body, though their function is not completely confirmed. The male has one such gland on each cheek which it uses to impress other males, attract females, and mark territorial boundaries. All other scent glands are found on both sexes—one at the base of each horn, one near the hock of each hind leg, one in the intersection of each cloven hoof, one near the center of the white rump patch, and a single gland on the lower back.

Although heading the other way, this buck can still keep a wary eye on the photographer. With such a wide choice of food in the area, he hesitated to leave.

Note the cloven hooves of this resting buck.

The hoof glands are supposedly effective in leaving a trail. The gland in the rump patch serves as a warning during an alarm, when the white hairs are flared out.

No warning, however, would be of any great value to the pronghorn if it could not escape from its enemies, and some of these are fast. Therefore, it has developed great speed. Various estimates place its top speed at 50 to 60 miles per hour, although anything over 55 is questionable. Some authorities not only claim that it is the fastest four-footed animal in North America, but that in the entire world only the African cheetah can run faster.

To gain speed, the ancestors of the pronghorn learned to run on their toes. The second and third toes were the longest and most used, so became well developed. The outer, unused toes gradually grew smaller and finally disappeared. Members of the deer family experienced much the same thing, but the outer toes have not completely disappeared. They remain on the back of each leg as small, useless protuberances called dewclaws. The horse runs on the tip of one toe, and is called an odd-toed ungulate, or hoofed animal. The pronghorn runs on two toe tips, so is called an even-toed ungulate. The cloven hooves are, in fact, its toenails.

A coyote takes off across the prairie.

The bottom of the pronghorn hoof is padded to withstand the pounding from the hard prairie surface or the occasional rock. The front hoof, which takes most of the beating when landing after a 12- or 25-foot bound, is a trifle larger than the rear hoof and more generously padded. Its edges are sharp and give a running pronghorn secure footing. It also acts as a weapon when the pronghorn is fighting a coyote or stomping a rattlesnake.

An individual wolf or coyote could never match the tremendous speed of the pronghorn. However, by setting up a relief runner to take over when the original attacker becomes tired, either predator could catch one. For example, a coyote may start a pronghorn running, chasing it in a definite direction where it is sure to pass another coyote, waiting to take over the chase. For this reason, the pronghorn needs endurance as well as speed. It has learned to run with its mouth open, thus gaining more air than would be possible through the nostrils alone. To accommodate this extra air, the windpipe is enlarged, or almost twice

the diameter of a man's. And, the lungs are much larger than in other animals of the same size.

Another aid to greater endurance is an enlarged heart, one almost twice the size of that of a sheep of equal weight. This allows extra blood that has been enriched with oxygen in the super lungs to be circulated through the arteries and veins to the needy muscles, replenishing energy and removing impurities quickly and efficiently. The combination gives the pronghorn the ability to outrun almost all its predators. It has been estimated to be able to maintain a constant 35 miles per hour over rough terrain for a distance of 5 or more miles.

Three dangerous periods in the lives of adult, wild animals are when they are resting, drinking, or feeding. When resting, most animals are lulled into a placid, less alert condition. When feeding or drinking, they are concentrating on the food or water; at either time, they can be approached by a predator more easily. With the exception of the lone buck that has left the herd because of age, pronghorns are too social to allow this to happen.

When a group of them lie down, every individual faces in a different direction. When feeding, each individual takes a bite, walks a few steps to another choice bit of food, and takes another

Six bucks rest and ruminate. As usual, they manage to see in all directions.

Mullein stalks dominate this patch of South Dakota prairie.

bite. During its short walk, it looks around the area, missing nothing. When each group member alternates biting with looking, there is never a time when at least one member is not on the alert for danger. They are often called nervous feeders. They are also called ruminants. Because of a multiple digestive system, they do not waste time chewing their food, exposed to possible enemies. Their four-compartment stomachs allow them to swallow and store unchewed roughage, until they can find a reasonably safe area, where they can lie down and chew their cuds in peace. Their stomachs are also equipped to handle foods which are unpalatable to most other prairie ruminants. In fact, pronghorns can exist on foods practically poisonous to other animals, such as thistles and cockleburs.

Seeing, smelling, or hearing an enemy may alert only one individual, but pronghorns use a system that warns the entire herd almost immediately. They do make sounds, and a sudden snort or coughlike call from one animal brings up the heads and

Pronghorns fleeing in any formation, their white rump hairs flared out in warning. These are running through Wyoming's sagebrush.

ears of all the members. At the same time, the rump glands discharge scent into the air. Some members of the herd may be beyond the odor and sound range of these warnings, but a third alarm system is effective for a mile or two.

The long, white rump hairs of the pronghorn are reasonably apparent for a great distance on even a relaxed animal. When a pronghorn becomes alarmed, the skin muscles contract and make every white hair on the rump stand straight out. This increases the size of the patch by several inches and its visibility to well over a mile for a human, and much farther for the pronghorn. An alarmed pronghorn snorts, flares its patch, and starts running, and every member of the herd responds by flaring its own patch and following the first animal. A frightened herd may run only a hundred yards or so before stopping and looking back. Although the first flight takes place instantly, with no definite leadership, the stop allows time to reassess the danger. If

A Montana herd flees in alarm. They have not yet stopped to regroup.

more running seems necessary, the pronghorns regroup, and take off. This second flight is normally led by a doe, with the other does and the young just behind, and the bucks bringing up the rear.

Newborn fawns are hard to find, but when discovered, remain perfectly still.

Young pronghorns are far more susceptible to predation than are older animals, and they too have special habits and adaptations to aid survival. They are born with little or no odor, and their sombre colors form a perfect camouflage against the prairie. Also, fawns, or kids, are helpless for only a day or so. They can stand and nurse within an average of thirty minutes. They can walk and even run a little in one hour, and a fawn can stay with the herd on the third day. Furthermore, the fawns are adept at hiding and are extremely difficult to find. They suckle frequently, but for only a few seconds at a time. Thus, like feeding adults, they are never exposed to danger for any length of time. The nursing mothers usually band together in small herds for mutual protection.

Pronghorn coats do not look heavy or warm enough for severe winter storms, especially when compared to the massive-looking coats of the bison. Yet they are. Although pronghorns do not have heavy fleece, they do have short, fine fur next to the skin, and each coarse, outer hair is a hollow, insulating tube. The same type of skin muscles that erect the hairs of the rump

The large, outer hairs of the pronghorn's coat are hollow, coarse, and brittle.

of an alarmed pronghorn also controls every hair on the body. When subzero north winds blow across the cold prairie, a very efficient mat of hairs tightly hugs the animal's body.

The pronghorn sheds twice a year, and the winter coat is composed of longer, heavier hairs to form this mat. In the spring, not only are these warmer hairs lost and replaced by shorter, lighter hairs, but the skin muscles relax and allow the hairs to separate and provide ventilation.

The pronghorn's large heart circulates blood in the slender legs, preventing them from freezing during an intense cold spell. The cold alone rarely destroys a pronghorn, but the chill factor caused by wind often can. Pronghorns have been known to survive temperatures of 40 degrees below zero on a calm day, but higher temperatures can destroy them when accompanied by strong winds. At zero degrees, a 20-mile wind brings a chill factor of minus 40 degrees. At 20 below zero—a common winter temperature on the high northern prairie—the same 20-mile wind brings the chill factor down to minus 68. To protect themselves from such winds, the pronghorns huddle behind the lee side of a hill or butte and, if caught on the open prairie, use tall sagebrush or some other dense, higher shrub for a windbreak.

3
Food and Feeding

All ruminants spend considerable time eating. They must. Plant life, which comprises all of their food, is low in concentrated fats and proteins, at least when compared to highly concentrated fish or meat diets.

Pronghorns spend more time feeding than most ruminants. It is their prime activity. They are dainty eaters and may cover several square miles of territory while sampling a bit of every type of plant the area offers. By moving while feeding, they protect themselves from predators better, and gain a far more nourishing, varied diet than mere grass could provide.

The pronghorn has no teeth on the front part of the upper jaw. Instead, it has a hard pad which the lower incisors meet when shearing off grass or weeds, or when stripping leaves and bark from shrubs. It has broad molars and premolars for grinding. Like all ruminants, the pronghorn has four compartments in its stomach, but the cecum, or storage area, is smaller than most. Its storage capacity is only two-thirds that of a sheep of equal weight. In fact, the entire stomach is about one-half the size of the sheep's. The small storage area, plus the pronghorn's habit of nibbling rather than stuffing, forces it to eat around the clock.

Tough plant fibers, or cellulose, are partially broken down by the chemical action of bacteria and protozoans within the rumen, the first of the stomach's divisions. The food then moves into the second compartment or reticulum (which with the rumen comprises the cecum), where the chemical treatment is

Left: *A feeding pronghorn.* Right: *Cud-chewing time for a staid old buck. The buck below is sampling weeds that grow in low areas, where water collects during showers.*

carried on further. With both areas filled, the pronghorn regurgitates a small quantity of the partially digested vegetation and chews its cud, as it is called, for about one or two minutes. The molars grind it into a pulpy mass, which is once more swallowed, but sent to the third compartment, or omasum, where gastric juices begin to break it down completely. This material is finally released into the abomasum, or fourth compartment where complete breakdown is finished. The speed of passage of the food through this system depends upon the toughness or chemical composition of what is eaten, but it usually takes twenty-four hours.

The pronghorn has a larger liver and kidneys than other ruminants of the same size. Many scientists believe these organs aid the pronghorn in digesting foods that prove somewhat toxic to other ruminants if eaten in any great quantity. It is known that the pronghorn consumes a large amount of sage. In fact, sage is the mainstay of its diet. Other ruminants, such as the deer and sheep, also eat sage, but only in small quantities. The sage, especially the big sagebrush, contains a higher percentage of fats, oils, proteins, sugars, and starches than most grasses and broad-leaved weeds called forbs. It is also somewhat toxic.

The liver of the pronghorn neutralizes the seleniums and alkaloids of plants high in these chemicals, and the enlarged kidneys collect and quickly pass these poisonous materials out of the body. The liver also stores sugar, the primary source of energy to animals. It turns the sugar into glycogen for storage and releases it as needed. Its large size in the pronghorn enables the animal to store more of this energy source, thereby increasing its endurance.

The pronghorn has another aid to digestion, which is lacking in the deer. It has a gallbladder, which stores the bile that is secreted by the liver. Bile is used in the breakdown of fats into more easily digested material. Grass and most plants have few or no fats in their tissues, but sage does.

Sage grows luxuriantly in among the prairie weeds and grasses.

It is believed, though not yet proved, that the bacteria and protozoans in the rumen and reticulum of the pronghorn are slightly different from those found in the digestive tracts of other ruminants. This could be another reason why the pronghorn can thrive on plants which are slightly toxic to most other ruminants.

A few typical plants eaten by pronghorns on various portions of their range, besides the sages (big Wyoming, dwarf, fringed, black and white, or silver), are juniper, rabbit brush, horse brush, snowberry, pasture sage, sweet clover, wild rose, goldenrod, sedges, wild lettuce, and parsley and several types of cactus, such as the pincushion and prickly pear. Unfortunately, pronghorns are prone to crawl under fences to get at the local farmer's field of flax, alfalfa, wheat, rye, and many other seasonal delicacies grown on the rangeland.

Sage, the preferred diet of the pronghorn, exists in all portions of its range, and a great amount of it is eaten throughout the year. In the spring, the fresh bark, shoots, and leaves are relished. In the summer, pronghorns continue to nibble on it as they pass by. In the winter, when snows have packed down and covered the dried forbs and grasses, they eat the larger, woodier

sagebrush that stands high over the snow cover. Whereas the drying of weeds and grasses makes them less nourishing, the dry winter sage retains much of its food value. It has been favorably compared to alfalfa as a food of high protein content in either summer or winter.

Like all living things, pronghorns need water. Most areas they frequent have a pond, lake, stream, or river within reach, which they visit about once each day. Watering places can be even more hazardous to prey animals than their feeding grounds. There may be only one place to get water over a huge part of the prairie, and all the animals may be forced to come to it for a drink. The predators are well aware of this, and are there too.

Pronghorns do not seem to require as much water as similar sized ruminants. They normally drink only one gallon in each twenty-four hours, or less, when water becomes scarce. During a drought, if their water sources all dry up, they may be forced to move to another location. During a prolonged drought, they may change their diet to succulent forbs which store water within their cells. Cactus pads store even more water than

Imagine biting into and eating the aptly named prickly pear. Pronghorns do!

succulents. They are eaten, often in considerable quantities, spines and all. Such a diet can sustain a pronghorn for long periods of time.

In the southwestern highlands, the resourceful pronghorns are believed to gain all their moisture needs from cactus and such weeds or forbs that store water from what little rainfall there is. They may never even have a drink from a stream or pond!

Food always seems to be available to the pronghorns, but occasionally they must travel in search of it. Either a portion of the range is dried up, or covered with snow too deep to walk in. If possible, the pronghorns seek new range. Some herds, if the local topography allows it, merely climb up the mountain slopes where the winds blow the snow cover off, or at least reduce it to where the animals can move around. Where there is no higher land nearby, they will migrate north or south, east or west—anywhere to find a new range where food or water is more accessible. These movements are not true migrations, because they occur only when necessary, are not very long, and usually end when conditions change.

4
Fawns and Baby-Sitters

Pronghorn territory is so vast that the springtime activities vary from one area to another. In the southern parts of the range, they begin a week or so earlier than in the northern parts. The elevation also affects the arrival of spring, because high country remains cooler longer than the lower areas. Over the central portions of their territory, where neither elevation nor temperature is extreme, the breakup of the large winter herds begins near the end of March. Instead of herds of twenty or sixty animals of all ages and both sexes, one now finds small bands of only four to six bucks together. Other little groups consist of yearling does and few, if any, older females. By now the pregnant does have left the herd and gone off alone, or in small groups of two or three, searching for adequate fawning grounds.

Near the end of April, the does begin to show both swollen abdomens and mammary glands. They have been seeking areas that have ample food, a source of water, and tall grasses, forbs, sagebrush, or other high shrubs to help hide their offspring.

Pronghorn does are dependable mothers. Almost all of them produce twins. So dependable are they that part of the state estimates of pronghorn numbers is based on the fact that every 100 does will produce approximately 180 fawns per season.

The actual birth and the next few hours of the life of a fawn are nothing short of marvelous. Pronghorn young are born into a threatening world of both severe weather conditions and many hungry predators. They are born out on the open prairie with

The bald eagle might take a fawn, but it is primarily a fish eater.

no shelter from either. Yet, except for extreme conditions, most of them survive.

The pronghorn gestation period is about eight months. By the end of this period, or the middle of May, the doe has located the best available area for having her young. Actual birth follows a labor lasting from two to four hours, during which time the doe alternates walking about, standing up, and lying down —but never leaves the chosen spot. The first of the twins is normally born while the doe is lying down. Almost immediately, the doe stands and begins to lick and clean the offspring, and is often still doing this when the twin makes its appearance. This second fawn is occasionally born while the doe is standing, and although it drops to the ground, it rarely seems to be injured in any way.

The licking and cleaning by the doe is done so thoroughly that its reasons have been questioned. Some think it is done to remove all birth scent from the fawn. Others say it is merely to

clean it as much as possible, while still others claim it is to establish an identity between mother and fawn. Perhaps the licking procedure accomplishes a bit of all three. There is no doubt that the warm fluid accompanying birth produces a scent that attracts predators. Eagles, bobcats, ravens, or coyotes try their best to locate and capture these newborn pronghorn antelope. They are especially hungry at this time, first because they have just been through the winter when food is often short, and second, they probably have young of their own that demand food.

Fawns weigh from $4\frac{1}{2}$ to 10 pounds at birth. Within five minutes they are wiggling about, attempting to get to their

A newborn fawn lies hidden in the grass.

mother's side. Within fifteen minutes or so they are standing, walking, and by one half-hour after birth, most of them are nursing. This rapid development is important to the fawns. Any number of does may be using the same area, and the combined odor of several sets of twins being born at about the same time is certain to draw predators. After being thoroughly cleaned by the doe's tongue, and dried off in the spring air, the fawns have little or no odor at all. However, the ground where they were born still retains considerable odor. Therefore, as soon as the fawns can follow, or two or more hours after birth, the doe leads them away from their place of birth to a fresh area.

Does stand up to nurse their young and arch their backs so the fawns can more readily reach the milk glands. A standing doe with two nursing fawns can easily be seen, so the pronghorn uses nursing periods which last only a few seconds. Although fawns may nurse for only forty seconds or so at a time, the milk they receive is highly concentrated. However, some have been seen nursing as often as eight times within the first three hours of life. The length of feeding time increases and the number of feedings decreases as the fawns grow older. By the third day, most fawns can outrun a man over rough prairie terrain and already have a good chance of escaping enemies.

A female pronghorn does not stay with her young for long periods of time as many other wild animal mothers do. After leading them away from the actual birth site, and after they have had several nursing periods, the doe may snort or grunt a command. It seems to be a command, because both fawns react to it by dropping to the ground and practically disappearing. It is amazing how obvious they are while nursing, and how completely they disappear when the command is given. They are there, and suddenly they are not! The mother now wanders off for a few yards and begins feeding. Meanwhile, neither fawn moves or even twitches an ear until their mother returns.

The young pronghorn is a drab, brownish-colored creature that matches the prairie ground and the surrounding grasses and weeds perfectly. It does not have the spots which are so prominent on deer fawns. Once hidden in what often seems an uncomfortable position, the fawn can practically be stepped on before it will move.

Even after the fawns have reached an age when they can run to some extent with their mother, should the doe grunt her command, they drop out of sight immediately, regardless of the terrain. Locating fawns on the wide expanse of shrub-dotted prairie is almost impossible.

After a short nursing period, the doe may wander off in search of food for herself. If there is no danger, the young may also wander off for a short distance and lie down. Twins rarely seek identical bedding places and may separate themselves by as much as 100 feet. Whatever the reason, it serves them well. A predator could conceivably locate one of them, yet be totally unable to find the second. If a fawn is ever closely threatened or attacked, its loud bleats bring any adult pronghorns within hearing distance dashing to the rescue.

After feeding, the doe returns to her young to allow them to

Left: *A doe looks for her fawn among the sagebrush.* Right: *Responding to its mother's mewing, a fawn comes out of hiding to be groomed.*

nurse. She returns directly to the area where she last saw the fawns and utters a low mew. The fawns dash out, the doe grunts an invitation, arches her back, and the fawns begin to nurse. Apparently the fawns soon learn to recognize the tone of their own mother's mew. There might be several does and young in the same immediate area, but observers believe that each fawn responds to its own mother's call.

Within a week or two, several sets of does and fawns join together and form a group. With them, there may also be some yearlings or last year's young. In this first grouping, or fawn group, the fawns are introduced into pronghorn society. They learn to recognize each other, plus the yearlings and does other than their own mothers.

After the fawns have met and begun to play with one another, the mothers often leave temporarily in search of some respite from their young. Occasionally, one doe will stay behind and seems to be filling the roll of a baby-sitter. The fawns often become so engrossed in their play that they never seem to miss their mothers, even if all of them wander off to feed or rest. Now and then one or more fawns will grow hungry and approach the first doe they see for milk. Normally, does will nose away all but

A doe leads her twins across the short-grass prairie.

Does, yearlings, and a single buck form a small herd.

their own offspring, but on occasion they have been seen nursing several fawns. A lone buck will often join such a fawn group, apparently providing extra protection.

Young pronghorns enjoy life! Each fawn is bubbling over with enthusiasm and is forever enticing others of the little group into their games. Such is their enthusiasm that even the does and the staid old buck that has joined the group find it hard to refuse, and occasionally join in the running, jumping, and games of follow-the-leader. The little ones soon begin challenging each other to shoving and pushing contests and rapidly gain both strength and agility. The does begin to refuse them nursing privileges, forcing them to nibble at the tender spring grasses or leaves of weeds and shrubs.

Pronghorn groups or herds have a well-established pecking order or hierarchy. Beginning in the fawn groups, each indi-

vidual does its best to establish itself as high in the hierarchy as possible. By the age of eleven weeks, the fawns have a basic knowledge of how high or low a position they hold in the pecking order. With female fawns, there is little change in the years to come. The position they win in the first eleven weeks is likely to be held throughout life. Due to the complicated breeding habits that come later, most males tend to contest their position in the hierarchy throughout much of their lives.

During the summer months, these small herds of does and fawns roam the immediate area, eating, resting, and occasionally mingling with other small groups. By late summer, the young does are well-established in their pecking order position; not only within their immediate group, but also with the other groups they have met. The young males, however, are still contesting their position with every new male they meet and are leaving the small herds of does to join other males of similar age. Almost all the doe fawns are weaned from their mothers by the end of August, but may still stay by their side. The young males mix with groups of bucks of all ages.

The so-called games of the fawns have really been contests of strength, agility, endurance, and spirit. They have learned to recognize each other by sight, smell, and ability. But now—late August—the time for play is over. Breeding time, or rut, is approaching!

5
Bucks, Does, and Harems

Unlike dogs, cats, horses, and most other animals, the pronghorns have a unique and complicated breeding program for which the males prepare from their earliest days. The end result of all the preparation is that only a few of the strongest, fastest, and most select bucks even have a chance at mating. Perhaps only six or seven bucks out of a sizable herd will breed with over 90 percent of the does. The remaining bucks, called bachelors, are just not strong, fast, aggressive, or good enough to compete successfully. A buck must be about three years of age before he gains sufficient weight and experience to challenge a ranking male successfully, although younger ones do try.

By the end of the first year, every male in the herd has a good idea of which bucks he can dominate, and which can dominate him. By the end of the second year, he knows. From this point on, until the actual breeding season begins, most confrontations between bucks are more bluff than fight. Although each one still tries to be superior, their confrontations usually stop short of actual battle.

The cheek glands on the head of a buck become more active, and the black hairs covering them become darker as the urge to breed increases. Cheek patch and scent displays are often enough to discourage a subordinate male. Other attitudes, such as stance, or lowering of the head in a threatening gesture, pawing the ground, or sometimes just a long stare, will prove to an antagonist that he is going to be dominant or fight, and the

A challenge—staring and presenting the cheek patch

The stare

lesser of the bucks will withdraw. Most such contests are bloodless, pushing contests. Some, however, become serious. The prong on the horns of a buck usually catches and deflects the other's thrusts; the skin around the head and neck of a buck is thicker and tougher than the skin of a doe. Still, the greater strength of the older buck is sometimes too much for a young challenger, and wounds or even death can result.

In the spring, when the winter herds break up, the dominant bucks begin to search for breeding territories. Some older bucks, that already have territories, return to them. These breeding areas are carefully chosen. Normally they are areas where forage is good, where the summer herds of does frequently feed. They must have access to water, and they need some obstruction like a bluff or river where they can corner their mates, not always cooperative during breeding season. These territories vary in size from a half-mile square to a full two miles square. The bucks that use and defend them are known as territorial bucks, and will use the same areas year after year, or until stronger bucks assume control. The new owners will not necessarily keep the same size territories, or the same boundaries.

All summer long the territorial bucks stay close to their chosen areas. They allow does and other bucks on their land, but as the breeding season grows closer, they become more belligerent. They are less inclined to let other bucks on, or even near, their territories.

Territorial bucks are quite obvious, although their territories are not—unless one spends many hours watching them. These bucks are the largest animals with the longest horns. Although they mingle with other bucks, they remain aloof, threatening and chasing away any that come too close. They have particular habits which, as summer progresses, become rituals. One is called thrashing. Now and then, these large bucks will be seen thrashing shrubs and bushes with their heads and horns, al-

A territorial buck

though no one seems to know what is accomplished.

Territorial bucks will paw the ground, stretch out and urinate on the hoof marks, then squat and defecate on the same spot. This ritual does serve a purpose. The odor marks the boundaries of the territory. Another marking device is chewing at the various shrubs and bushes along the area boundaries, and rubbing the cheek glands on the twigs. Only constant watching of a territorial buck will reveal the outline of a territory for a human, whereas pronghorns, of course, can smell these markings.

Although bucks are ready to breed about anytime during the summer, does are receptive only for about two weeks. This estral period, as it is called, falls between the last two weeks of

September and the first two of October, depending on the geographic location. As this time approaches, the large males become more and more aggressive toward the nonterritorial bachelors. Large bachelors with no suitable breeding areas may attempt to take one already occupied, and more and more fights occur. A no-man's-land grows up between and around established territories. This is where the bachelors roam. The breeding bucks remain on their own land, defending it from all other bucks. Occasionally, two territories lie side by side and the owner bucks set up mutual boundaries by a method known as a parallel walk. Each male remains on his own land and walks parallel to the other buck. Both stop now and then for the urination-defecation marking procedure, and each thrashes and gland-marks the shrubs on his own side of the line.

The does continue to roam wherever they wish, seemingly indifferent to the battles raging around them. However, they have been watching, because when their estral period arrives they are definitely choosy about which male they will mate with. When the estral period of the does begins, the entire herd is involved in a display of frantic activity surrounding the terri-

A group of bachelor bucks on no-man's-land

A group of does

tories of the dominant males.

The established territories are actually harems, but as yet, without does. These, the bucks must seek out. The large, non-

A territorial buck and his harem

territorial males continue either to contest the territorial bucks, or try to steal their does. The locating and driving of the selected mates, the fighting of competitive males, and the recovery of stolen mates keep each territorial buck on the run for the full two weeks of the rutting season.

Some of the large bucks mark out such a large breeding area that they can hardly keep bachelor males off their property, or the does on it. These same bucks may be prone to selecting too many does. The bucks that mark out a medium-sized breeding area, and select a group of three or four does, have a much less trying season.

When the does become receptive to the males, they exude an entirely different odor from the normal. This odor excites the males which approach them in an effort to mount and breed them. The large harem masters are busy rounding up such does, and with gentle butting and lots of footwork, guide or drive them onto their breeding territories. Some does, although not willing, are driven anyhow. These may run off the area as soon as the buck leaves to fight, chase away another buck, or perhaps to round up another mate.

Right up until the estral period begins and the rutting season is in full swing, the does over two years of age wander freely on the range. Each little doe group, with its following of female yearlings, stays reasonably close to its home territory. When rut begins, and both bachelor and territorial bucks start chasing the females, the small doe herds break up and the individual females run from territory to territory, and all over the no-man's-land.

Most bucks with breeding areas attempt to drive the does to their own harem whether the does are willing or not. Bachelor bucks begin courting the females wherever they can. The does flee from undesirable contacts and stand for those males they favor. Although nonterritorial bucks attempt courtship with

The dominant buck on the left forces up a "bedding" buck.

The bedding buck offers a show of resistance, but finally walks away.

free-running does, the harem bucks, constantly crisscrossing the entire area, are almost certain to see and chase them away.

Courtship in pronghorn society is a mutual agreement. Both male and female must be acceptable to each other. The territorial buck approaches the doe with head held high, ears erect, and with a prancing gait. He stands close to the doe and stares directly at her. If the doe does not run or walk away, but stares back at him, he offers his cheek patch gland to sniff. Her tail is then erected and the buck pushes his chest against her rump. If the doe still stands, the buck mounts her by standing on his hind legs and resting his forelegs on her back.

Should a buck approach an unwilling doe, she either walks or runs away. If the buck becomes insistent, the doe merely twists her head back and forth in a negative manner, and the harem buck normally stops and walks away. Occasionally a doe, seeing a large harem buck nearby, will start the courtship by raising her tail and staring at him intently.

Bachelor bucks approach does in the same manner as the harem bucks do, but are frequently refused by the does who are either not ready, or prefer the larger harem buck's attention. These bucks, having no harem, persist in their attentions, and unless driven away by a territorial buck, will chase a doe for miles. Often, if the doe becomes sufficiently tired, she will give in.

The end of the two-week rutting season comes suddenly. One day the entire breeding area is alive with running, fighting, courting, and mating pronghorns, and the next day there is little or no activity. The does are either bred and have no more desire for contact, or with the end of the estral period, the exciting odor of this period no longer affects the males. Little by little, the scattered females begin to join the bachelor and territorial males to form the large winter herds. The yearlings and

Winter herds begin to form in the fall.

fawns break up their peer herds to mingle with the winter herds. All the fighting, chasing, and bickering stops until the next year, and only a show of bluff now and then proves that the pecking order still exists.

6
Pronghorn Problems

The problems that the prehistoric pronghorn faced must be guessed at, but they are educated guesses. One would be the fierce predators that roamed this continent thousands of years ago—the dire wolves, the saber-toothed tigers, or the large, meat-eating reptiles. It was probably due to them that the pronghorn developed its tremendous running speed, endurance, and oversized organs. Another would be the Ice Age, when the world cooled down until much of the land was under great ice flows or glaciers. These conditions lasted for thousands of years.

The earliest observed problems were related to predators—the great wolf packs, grizzly bears, and mountain lions. All these are mentioned in the journals of the early explorers of North America. Then in 1873, a disease of epidemic proportions destroyed an estimated 75 percent or more of the pronghorns found between the Yellowstone and Missouri rivers. This may be the only record of such wholesale destruction by disease, but we can assume that it could have happened at other times and places.

Also documented was an especially severe winter storm over much of North America which destroyed thousands of pronghorns. This also must have happened before, and in other places, but by 1893—when this storm struck—most of the great buffalo herds had already been exterminated. Before, when great storms laid a heavy blanket of snow over the prairie, the tremendous weight and strength of the buffalo enabled them to

Bison and pronghorns have shared the same range throughout their history.

push through the drifts to the feeding areas. After a million such massive, living snowplows had trampled down the snow, the lighter, smaller pronghorn had little trouble following, if not mingling with, the buffalo to reach adequate food. Now, with the huge buffalo herds gone, much less snow stopped the pronghorn.

One of the most inescapable, widespread, and recurring problems of the pronghorn is the spring storms that might strike at any portion of the high, northern range. The fawns are born in May, and these storms can hit as late as June. The spring grass can be green and succulent; the bushes, forbs, and shrubs leafed out; the weather seasonable and beautiful. Suddenly, with little or no warning, the weather turns cold, the north winds begin to blow, and the snow flies with all the vigor of a midwinter blizzard. Should such a storm reach an area soon after the fawns are

born, they will die. There is little shelter on the wide open prairie from the chilly winds or blowing, drifting snow, especially when the newborn animals can barely walk. Almost every year some portion of pronghorn range undergoes such a one- to three-day spring blizzard, and most of the fawns of that area die. Adults, too, sometimes die in spring storms, especially if weakened by inadequate food during a severe winter.

Hunters alone may not have reduced the pronghorn herds, but they have helped. In some areas, like Baja California, parts of Mexico, Arizona, and New Mexico, the inadequate rainfall has reduced pronghorn country to desert. The sparse vegetation can only support small herds, and when uncontrolled hunting is permitted, an entire population could easily be destroyed.

Drought, if persistent, can cause a major problem for pronghorns. On the northern plains, under normal conditions, there is more than enough food for thousands of them. However, after a year or two of drought, much of it is gone. The pronghorns are forced to migrate, but if the drought covers a wide area, there may be no place to go. Many will die. Also, during long droughts, there may be only one or two water holes in thousands

A doe in winter pelage. She has not yet completed her spring shedding.

of acres. All the animals in the area assemble at these places, including the predators, and the surrounding vegetation is further devastated by the concentration of the plant-eating animals.

Pronghorns have benefited from civilization by a reduction in predators. The farmers and ranchers shot out the wolves, lions, and bears. They also reduced the eagle population, and are still attempting to rid the prairie of the coyote. The pronghorns help themselves to water from the stock dams, and lick the salt blocks set out for cattle. During the snowy months of winter, they also follow the trails that ranchers make across the prairie to reach their snowbound stock. Pronghorns then help themselves to the hay or alfalfa left for the domestic animals. In the spring, they crawl through or under the barbed wire fences and nibble on the newly sprouted grains that farmers have planted. They also benefit from laws controlling the hunting of pronghorns.

Civilization has brought problems, however. With sheep, cattle, and horses came thousands of miles of barbed wire to contain them. Roads and railroads divided the land. Men constructed stock dams and raised crops, all of which forced the wide-ranging, fast-running pronghorn to change its way of life.

For thousands of years, pronghorns had been able to run as

Pronghorns, oil wells, fences, and sage in eastern Wyoming

Three pregnant does cross the highway in search of a good fawning area.

fast and as far as they desired. They could run around any obstacle, though they can jump. In their play, they have been seen making jumps which are far higher than needed to clear any western stock fence. A few have been seen actually jumping fences as easily and as gracefully as any deer. Basically, however, pronghorns prefer to slide under fences or crawl through them. Either way, the barbs can inflict ugly wounds. Furthermore, when a frightened herd is running fast, their eyes can be watching the far hills they are running for, and not see the thin strands of wire across their path. Pronghorns, under these conditions, occasionally pile up into a fence, injuring or even killing themselves.

Pronghorns will associate with cattle and horses but, somehow, they care less for sheep. However, they do enter areas where sheep have grazed, and they are susceptible to stock-carried diseases. In fact, all ruminants can be infected with either round or flat intestinal worms. Such internal parasites are passed from animal to animal through the feces. The sheep or cattle droppings on the ground can contain the egg stages of the worms, and the next animal to eat the grass or weeds of that area

Pronghorns freely associate with cattle.

can easily swallow them and become infected itself. Cattle and sheep concentrated in fenced areas create a great problem.

Infected domestic stock animals are treated by the owner for both external and internal parasites, either with medicines, dips, or sprays, but the wild pronghorn is on its own. In late 1976, an unusually high death rate of pronghorn antelope of eastern Wyoming was traced to a sheep disease called "blue tongue." It is caused by a virus carried by insects, and although the sheep could be treated, many pronghorns died. Pronghorns mingling with large herds of domestic animals are much more readily infected now than ever before.

Normally, the eating habits of pronghorns produce very little damage to the rangeland. Because they eat so little grass and so many weeds, shrubs, and sage, they usually don't compete that much with cattle and sheep. But there are times when feeding pronghorns do become such a nuisance that landowners will not tolerate any more of them in their area. After several years of good rainfall, normal temperatures, and protective laws, prong-

horns multiply tremendously. If drought conditions begin, or there is merely less moisture, then the grass and weed crop is reduced and is not as succulent. The choice food is limited, and pronghorns become competitive with domestic stock. They begin to crawl through the farmer's fences to eat his crops, especially if they are being grown on an irrigated field.

This is the point at which local farmers and ranchers begin to demand that more hunting licenses be issued. The control officers seldom argue too much about this. They have already flown slowly over the area in low-flying planes, counting and estimating the number of pronghorns in their district. They have walked over the land to see the condition of the prairie grasses. They have inspected the farmer's fields for signs of destruction.

This count, no matter how carefully made, is subject to change. Along the borders of the pronghorn states, there is always a fluctuation as pronghorns travel first to one state and then back. During droughts or winter storms, entire herds of fifty or more may pass over a border for a stay of only a few weeks. Considering that some of the common borders of the western states are hundreds of miles long, these moves can make a tremendous difference.

Because the pronghorn is the last of the plentiful, free-running big game in North America, and because of the interest in them on the part of hunters, ecologists, and people who enjoy

A postage stamp issued in 1956, which featured the pronghorn antelope

A handsome pronghorn buck on the move

wildlife, there is little chance of the North American pronghorn ever becoming extinct. Their open, free country may be cut down in size and their numbers may change from time to time as severe winters, droughts, or diseases come and go. But after surviving the tremendous changes that time has brought on, they can certainly cope with the future—especially with our assistance.

Bibliography

Anthony, H. E. 1928. *Field Book of North American Mammals.* New York and London: Putnam's.

Autenrieth, Robert E. and Ficter, Edson. March, 1975. *On the Behavior and Socialization of Pronghorn Fawns.* A Wildlife Monograph. The Idaho Fish and Game Department and Idaho State University.

Carrington, Richard. 1963. *Mammals.* Life Nature Library. New York: Time-Life.

Farb, Peter. 1966. *The Land and Wildlife of North America.* Life Nature Library. New York: Time-Life.

Grzimek's Animal Life Encyclopedia. 1968. New York: Van Nostrand.

Interstate Antelope Conference. 1962 Transactions. P.O. Box 1551, Reno, Nevada.

Kitchen, David W. 1974. *Social Behavior and Ecology of the Pronghorn.* A Wildlife Monograph. Louisville, Ky.: University of Louisville.

Kohler, Paul Harold. 1950. Digestion Studies with Sheep and Wild Antelope on a Sagebrush Ration. Thesis. Brookings, S.D.: South Dakota State College.

McClung, Robert M. 1969. *Lost Wild America.* New York: Morrow.

Mace, Robert U. 1949. Revised 1954. *Oregon's Pronghorn Antelope.* Oregon State Game Commission, 1634 S.W. Alder St., Portland, Oreg.

O'Hara, Cleophas C. 1920. *The White River Badlands.* Rapid City, S.D.: School of Mines and Technology.

Orr, Robert T. 1971. *Mammals of North America.* Garden City, N.Y.: Doubleday.

Popowski, Bert. 1959. *Hunting Pronghorn Antelope.* Harrisburg, Pa.: Stackpole.

Prenzlow, E. J., Bilbert, D. L., and Glover, F. A. June, 1968. Special Report #17. *Some Behavior Patterns of the Pronghorns.* Colorado Department of Game, Fish and Parks.

Romer, Alfred S. 1941. *Man and the Vertebrates.* 3rd ed. Chicago: University of Chicago Press.

Sundstrom, Charles, Hepworth, William G., and Dien, Kenneth L. 1973. Bulletin #12. *Abundance, Distribution and Food Habits of the Pronghorn.* Cheyenne, Wyo.: Wyoming Game and Fish Commission.

Index

G. EARL CHACE lives in Rapid City, South Dakota, where he has been Curator of the Black Hills Reptile Gardens for over twenty years. Aside from his work at the Gardens, Mr. Chace is also an instructor on poisonous reptiles, arachnids, and insects for the Emergency Medical Training courses of the South Dakota State Department of Health. He is the author of numerous magazine articles, a weekly nature column for the Rapid City *Journal,* and *Wonders of Rattlesnakes* and *Wonders of Prairie Dogs* in this series.